BREEDERS' BE
A KENNEL CLUB BOOK

P9-BIT-917

Pug

By Anna Katherine Nicholas

BREEDERS' BEST
A KENNEL CLUB BOOK™

PUG

ISBN: 1-59378-917-3

Copyright © 2004
Kennel Club Books, LLC
308 Main Street, Allenhurst, NJ 07711 USA
Printed in South Korea

ALL RIGHTS RESERVED. NO PART OF THIS BOOK MAY BE REPRODUCED IN ANY FORM,
BY PHOTOSTAT, SCANNER, MICROFILM, XEROGRAPHY OR ANY OTHER MEANS, OR
INCORPORATED INTO ANY INFORMATION RETRIEVAL SYSTEM, ELECTRONIC OR
MECHANICAL, WITHOUT THE WRITTEN PERMISSION OF THE COPYRIGHT OWNER.

10 9 8 7 6 5 4 3 2

PHOTOS BY:
Isabelle Français,
Carol Ann Johnson
and Bernd Brinkmann.

DRAWINGS BY:
Yolyanko el Habanero.

Contents

Meet the Pug

Over time, there have been varying ideas about the origin of the quaint little dog known as the Pug, but it is generally accepted that the breed originated in China. From there the Pug spread into Japan and later to Europe where, while remaining a pure breed, it was also crossed with some longer-faced European breeds and so now lies in the ancestry of several other breeds. Yes, this is indeed a breed with history!

In ancient China, dogs were treated like royalty, and some Pugs today still get the royal treatment!

It is likely that China's Ha-pa Dog is the Pug's near ancestor. The Ha-pa Dog, a breed that is hardly known outside its homeland, in appearance resembles a smooth-coated Pekingese. "Short-mouthed" dogs have probably been known in China since around 1115 BC, and there are records of them dating as far back as 663 BC.

All Pugs agree that this is an enchanting, playful, good-humored breed with a fascinating history.

Although attitudes in China are now sadly very different, there was a time when dogs were treated almost like royalty. Some were given titles of rank, they had their own servants to care for their every need and they were carefully guarded. Pugs care not whether their owners are rich or poor, just as long as they are loved and cared for, but at one time they were owned mainly by people of high rank. It seems that many of them were treated more as ornaments than as dogs! The Pug enjoyed such popularity

The Pug is a toy breed with a substantial frame for his small size.

until the 12th century and possibly beyond, but by the 16th century, interest had waned.

The Pug seems to have come to Europe via Russia, where many were kept by the aunt of Catherine the Great. When the breed arrived in Europe, it was much like the was known as the "Dutch Mastiff." It is important to recall that the Dutch East India Company played a significant trading role with the Orient, and it is certain that both Pugs and Pekingese came back to Europe on its ships.

In 1688 William of Orange came to England with his wife

The Pekingese is a fellow short-faced breed of China.

Pug we know today, though its distant ancestors were probably mastiffs and the ancient fighting dogs of Greece.

In Holland the Pug has been especially popular and there it

Mary, and they brought several Pugs with them, each wearing an orange ribbon around its neck. Interestingly enough, a Pug is credited with saving the life of William's great-grandfather, William the Silent. One jumped onto the prince's face to waken him when under the threat of surprise attack from Spanish troops in 1572.

do ladies were out walking, it was not unusual to see them with a turbaned servant and also a Pug. Someone especially fond of the breed in that era

The Chinese Shar-Pei shares a country of origin with the Pug, and the two breeds share some wrinkles, too.

In England the breed soon became popular and in early days was known as the "Dutch Pug," only later taking the name Pug or "Pug-dog." It was highly fashionable in 18th-century Britain; when well-to-

was Charlotte, wife of King George III. However, by the end of the reign of George IV in 1830, the Pug was no longer in fashion, and within just a few short years the Pug had fallen into serious decline.

How lucky are British Pug lovers today that that eminent lady, Queen Victoria, was a fan of the breed; once royalty found the breed in favor again, others followed suit. It seems that her original Pugs were given to her by relations along the Continent, and hers were kept primarily as nursery dogs, for they got along so well with the children. Another royal dog-lover, Queen Alexandra, was also a devotee of the breed, her husband having given her one before departing for a tour of India.

Traditionally a favorite with the ladies, the Pug still attracts many a female fancier!

In Britain there were two main strains in the early part of the 19th century, but these lines finally came together and, in doing so, lost their individuality. There are varying stories surrounding some of the early importations. Two might possibly have come from a Russian tightrope walker, but it is also possible that a Hungarian countess living in Vienna may have had something to do with it! There is a story of others' having been captured during the siege of China's Summer Palace.

Fawn and apricot were the colors originally known in the Pug, and in 1877 black was considered a "new" color in the breed. But be this as it may, black was certainly known before then, for William Hogarth painted one in the

1700s. There is a theory that blacks that had been bred in England from fawns and apricots were considered mutations, and in consequence were destroyed at birth. However, it is also possible that those "blacks" were not true blacks, but smuts, so their color was not thought to be attractive.

The Pug has long been depicted in art. Aside from Hogarth, Goya and Reinagle are two well-known artists whose names immediately spring to mind. The Pug has also been featured in porcelain and on snuff bottles, tobacco jars and paperweights. Those interested in Freemasonry may be fascinated to know that in 18th-century Germany a Pug was portrayed by the Freemasons to denote a symbol of stubbornness when followers were excommunicated by the Pope. This is the reason that the Pug frequently appears on Meissen porcelain. In Germany the Freemasons functioned underground as *Mopsorden*, meaning "The Order of Pugs," and in fact in many countries today the Pug is still known by the name "Mops."

The Pug is "classically" popular around the world!

Fawn, shown here, and apricot were the colors known in the Pug during the breed's early development.

In 1877 the black coloration was considered new in the breed, but black Pugs certainly existed before that time.

In England the first breed club was approved by the Kennel Club in 1883. In America the first Pugs arrived not long after the Civil War, and the breed was accepted by the American Kennel Club in 1885.

At the time of their AKC acceptance, Pugs were actively shown throughout the US. The breed's popularity waned in the next few decades, but dedicated fanciers kept enough interest alive so that by 1931 it was decided that a breed club should be formed. The Pug Dog Club of America was established in 1931 by a group of Pug devotees on the East Coast; the club was recognized by the AKC later that same year.

Since those times, the Pug has enjoyed consistent popularity in the US. In fact, recent AKC registration statistics place the Pug in the top 20 most popular breeds. This endearing little breed is loved and cherished all over the world, and very deservedly so.

MEET THE PUG

Overview

- The Pug's origins are widely accepted as beginning in China, with that country's Ha-pa Dog as a close ancestor.
- In its early days in China the Pug was treated like royalty, although the breed's popularity declined between the 12th and 16th centuries.
- The breed arrived in Europe, likely via Russia, and became especially popular in Holland and England.
- Interesting facts about the Pug's history can be gleaned from the breed's appearance in artwork.
- The Pug has experienced ups and downs in the US but has enjoyed a constant level of popularity since the inception of the breed club. It is now one of America's best-loved breeds.

Description of the Pug

The Pug displays great charm and dignity, befitting his ancestry, and he also has a lively disposition and is a happy dog of even temper. These qualities make the Pug a thoroughly adorable companion. His characteristic good looks are just as enchanting as his endearing personality.

Ideally a Pug weighs only 14–18 lb (6.3–8.1 kg) but is described in the breed standard as *multum in parvo*, an expression from ancient Latin that can be translated as "a lot in a little." Most fanciers agree that this description of the Pug is

Who can resist this face? This Pug exhibits a lovely head, with large eyes, a dark mask, typical wrinkles and the correct undershot bite, all contributing to the breed's signature expression.

12

right on target. This is shown in the breed's compactness of form, well-knit proportions and hardness of muscle. The Pug is decidedly square and cobby, with a large, round head and short, blunt, square muzzle. The wrinkles on the head and face are clearly defined, the American breed standard's stating that they are "large and deep." The dark eyes are large and globular in shape, with a soft and solicitous expression; when the Pug is excited, however, his eyes are full of fire! A Pug's mouth is slightly undershot, the jaw wide, with the incisor teeth almost in a straight line. Although many judges do not inspect the inside of a Pug's mouth, it is undesirable for the mouth to be wry or for the teeth or tongue to be showing.

All lined up! Pugs are popular show dogs, attracting large entries and many fascinated spectators.

Toy breeds are stacked on a table for evaluation in the show ring, bringing them closer to the judge and enabling a full hands-on examination.

The small ears are thin and soft, like black velvet, but two kinds of ear are correct for the Pug, the "rose" and the "button," the latter being preferred. The rose ear is a small drop ear that folds over and back to reveal the burr; in the button ear, the ear flap folds forward with the tip lying close to the skull to cover the opening.

All aspects of the Pug's head combine to make this one of the breed's most memorable traits. His head is just brimming with character, set on a strong, thick neck with sufficient length to carry the head proudly. And that face! His short muzzle, furrowed brow and large gentle eyes create an expression like no other in dogdom. Everybody recognizes a Pug!

The Pug's body is short and cobby. The chest is wide and well ribbed with a topline that is level. In keeping with this sturdy little breed, the forelegs are strong, straight and of moderate length, and the shoulders are well sloped. The back legs, too, are strong, with a good turn of stifle. They should be straight and parallel when viewed from behind. Although the American standard varies little from the British and European standards, it adds a descriptive phrase, stating that the "thighs and buttocks are full and muscular." This just serves to typify the breed, adding to its overall cobby appearance.

A Pug does not have cat-like feet, but he also should not have feet that are as long as those of the rabbit. The toes are well split up and the nails should be black. When the dog is moving, the feet should point directly to the front, turning neither in nor out. Dewclaws on the Pug are generally removed. When moving, a slight roll of the hindquarters typifies the Pug's gait, which is free, self-assured and jaunty.

So now we come to the tail, and who can forget this

Left: Correct head and facial expression with desirable rose ear. Right: Incorrect ear shape and carriage; muzzle too narrow.

Left: Profile showing body in proper proportions with correct tail set and carriage. Right: Faults: Chest too deep, protruding forechest, incorrect set and carriage of ears and tail.

Left: Desirable tightly curled tail. Right: Fault: Tail not tightly curled.

Left: Correct forequarters with good width of chest and straight legs. Right: Faults: Narrow chest; turning in at hocks.

Occiput: Upper back part of skull; apex.

Skull: Cranium.

Stop: Indentation between the eyes at point of nasal bones and skull.

Muzzle: Foreface or region of head in front of eyes.

Lips: Fleshy portion of upper and lower jaws.

Flews: Hanging part of upper lip.

Withers: Highest part of the back, at the base of neck above the shoulders.

Shoulder: Upper point of forequarters; the region of the two shoulder blades.

Forechest: Sternum.

Chest: Thoracic cavity (enclosed by ribs).

Forequarters: Front assembly from shoulder to feet.

Upper arm: Region between shoulder blade and forearm.

Elbow: Region where upper arm and forearm meet.

Forearm: Region between elbow and wrist.

Carpus: Wrist.

Dewclaw: Extra digit on inside of leg; fifth toe.

Brisket: Lower chest.

Topline: Outline from withers to tailset.

Back: Dorsal surface, extending from the withers.

Loin: Lumbar region between ribs and pelvis.

Body: Region between the fore- and hindquarters.

Stern: Tail.

Croup: Pelvic region; rump.

Hip: Joint of pelvis and upper thigh bone.

Hindquarters: Rear assembly from pelvis to feet.

Upper thigh: Region from hip joint to stifle.

Stifle: Knee.

Lower thigh: Hindquarter region from stifle to hock; second thigh.

Flank: Region between last rib and hip.

Hock: Tarsus or heel.

Abdomen: Surface beneath the chest and hindquarters; belly.

Pastern: Region between heel (or wrist) and toes.

Digit: Toe.

CHAPTER 2

lovely high-set tail, curled as tightly as possible over the hip? Indeed a double curl is highly appreciated. Can you imagine a Pug with an uncurled tail? Just like his unforgettable face, the curled tail is one of the Pug's hallmark characteristics.

The Pug has a fine, smooth, soft coat that is short and glossy. It should not be harsh or woolly. The breed comes in four colors, silver, apricot, fawn and black. These colors are clearly defined, as are the markings on the muzzle or mask, ears, moles on the cheeks and thumb-mark or diamond on the forehead. From the upper back point of the skull to the twist of the tail, there is a trace that should be as dark as possible.

Now that you have a detailed physical description

The Pug has a short, compact, cobby body with his tail curled over his back.

of the Pug, let's discuss the huge personality packed inside that compact body. The Pug is nothing short of delightful. He is a good-tempered, playful, inquisitive, even clownish character with a wonderful sense of humor. That being said, he also retains an air of dignity. Bred as companion dogs, Pugs thrive on interaction with their humans and do not enjoy being left alone. They want to be true members of the family and are happiest when included in everything that their owners do. Since the Pug is a true charmer, most owners feel the same way, enjoying their Pugs' companionship wherever they go. Fortunately, the breed's small size makes traveling with a Pug convenient.

So now you have an image of the Pug in a nutshell, and what a remarkable little character he is, *multum in parvo* (a lot in a little) indeed!

DESCRIPTION OF THE PUG

Overview

- *Multum in parvo* is an expression coined in the breed standard to aptly describe the Pug as "a lot in a little," both physically and in personality.
- The head is the breed's most noticeable hallmark, as the short muzzle, facial wrinkles, inquisitive dark eyes and undershot bite combine to create an unforgettable expression.
- The Pug's body is described as "cobby," square and compact.
- Another of the breed's trademarks is the curled tail.
- The Pug's good humor and love of his owner's companionship, along with his convenient size, have endeared him to many a fancier.

CHAPTER 3

Are You a Pug Person?

Pugs are wonderful companions. They thrive on being included in their owners' activities and enjoy hanging out with friends.

If you have a clown-like personality and a puckish sense of humor, you will have much in common with your Pug. This is a breed that can provide endless hours of amusement and will be only too happy for you to join in with his fun and games. Whether you live a sedentary lifestyle or a rather more active one, you can be sure that your Pug will fit in.

As an owner in the more active category, you will enjoy taking your Pug for short walks. As this is a short-

nosed breed, you should always keep an eye on the weather. Don't allow your dog to get too hot. Be prepared to make stops along the way and take caution if your Pug starts breathing heavily. It is always a good idea to carry along a supply of drinking water to quench your Pug's thirst when walking and exercising.

If your Pug gets winded or starts to pant, give him ample opportunity to rest.

For a Pug, simple games in the fenced yard are good fun and will help to exercise those muscles. It is important to remember that although your Pug is only a "little person" (in more ways than one), he will need some regular exercise. Of course, he will want you to join him in this.

The Pug as water retriever? Not by trade, but dogs of many breeds enjoy swimming if properly and safely introduced to water.

If you are as much fun as your Pug, then you will have a happy, lively disposition. Though even-tempered, you probably carry a bit of a stubborn streak, which means that you can be strong-willed. Although you enjoy meeting people and show an outward friendliness toward strangers, it really is your nearest and dearest that you love the most! You are quite fearless by nature, which can sometimes get you into a bit of trouble, but you are certainly not aggressive (although you might just show a little temper when jealousy rears its head). In truth, you love warmth and affection and will accept as much as you can get. If all of these aforementioned personality traits apply to you, then you and your Pug are almost blood brothers already! Pugs are known to thrive on their humans' affection and can never get enough companionship.

If there are children in your life, you will have to teach them to respect the

In Germany, where the breed name is "Mops," these pampered Pugs travel in style in their very own "Mops Mobil."

little figure of canine comedy that has entered your home and family. In

Maybe you want a competent watchdog but have neither the space nor

The "little person" known as the Pug will befriend the other little people in the home. Introductions between children and dogs should always be supervised for the best interest of all concerned.

general, Pugs seem to show special affection toward children, but you must take care that tiny fingers do not get poked into your Pug's gloriously globular eyes. Always remember that however good a dog's temperament, his patience should never be tested to its limits.

physical strength to take on one of the giant breeds, in which case maybe the Pug is just the breed for you. Although small in stature, the Pug has a surprisingly deep bark and can certainly give potential intruders the impression that a much larger dog is inside guarding your house! The Pug is always ready to give a good bark when the doorbell rings, so if you are a little hard of hearing, you can be sure your Pug will let you know if a visitor has arrived.

On a negative note, if you hate a sleeping

The black Pug possesses a beautiful velvety coat that positively shines.

companion who snores, then you may want to think about having a different breed. Many Pugs enjoy a good snore during their slumber time, though there

are some exceptions. However, on a positive note, if you don't appreciate doggy odors around your home, then the Pug may be a good choice. If kept clean, Pugs are usually virtually free from such smells.

As for grooming, you probably like to look your best, though perhaps you feel you were not exactly cut out to be a hairstylist. Not to worry, the Pug's coat doesn't demand much attention, at least not in comparison with his abundantly coated Chinese cousin, the Pekingese. Pugs do shed all year round. While regular brushing will remove dead hairs, Pug owners still should be prepared to find little clouds around the house, on clothes and on furniture. This is normal, but excessive shedding likely indicates a problem that you should discuss with your veterinarian.

And finally, I'm not suggesting that you are greedy, but if you have a healthy appetite, you will have something else in common with your Pug! Most Pugs really enjoy their food and thus are prone to putting on too much weight. This means that you will need to take fairly strict control of his diet but, when all is said and done, it's usually easier to start a diet and exercise plan when your companion is on one, too!

The Pug is popular for his sweet temperament, irresistible expression and charming sense of humor.

ARE YOU A PUG PERSON?

Overview

- The Pug's clownish personality, playful nature and adaptability make him a fun companion in whatever you do.
- Pug owners must take caution, as short-faced breeds are more prone to breathing problems, heat stroke and other health issues.
- The Pug may be a little stubborn, but never aggressive and certainly always good-natured.
- The Pug owner does not need to be a professional groomer, but must be prepared to keep the Pug's short coat in top condition.
- Weight control is an issue with Pugs, as they certainly enjoy eating and need their owners to set healthy limits.

Selecting a Pug Breeder

The Pug is an endearing little character who has come to be loved in many corners of the world. This means that there are a considerable number of breeders, so you should not encounter too much difficulty in locating one. That being said, while it will not be too difficult to locate a Pug breeder, it will take a little more time and research on your part to find a responsible breeder, the only kind of breeder from whom you should consider obtaining a pup. You must be as certain as you possibly can be

A Pug is a charming addition to almost any home. What excitement comes along with adding a Pug to your family!

that the breeder you find is an ethical and reputable protector of this very special breed.

If you hope to have a Pug to take into the show ring, you may need to have your name included on a waiting list until such time as a puppy with show potential becomes available. Even if you have no intentions of showing, you still may have to wait for an available puppy from the breeder of your choice. If you choose your breeder wisely, the wait will be worth it.

It's hard to resist bringing home a whole basketful of Pug puppies, but don't let yourself get swept away! Use your head to make a wise decision.

Prospective puppy buyers should always keep foremost in their minds that there are many different kinds of breeder, some with the breed's best interest at heart, others less dedicated and more profit-motivated. It is essential that you locate one who not only has dogs that you admire but also breeding ethics with which you

You are seeking a breeder who loves the breed, participates in the breed club and activities with her dogs and makes bettering the breed the top priority in her breeding program.

can agree. Sadly, in all breeds there are invariably some who are simply "in it for the money," and these you must give a wide berth.

That said, there are many good breeders around. If you look carefully, you will find just such a person. If you can be personally recommended, that is perhaps ideal. Introducing yourself to Pug people at a dog show is a good place to start; additionally, you should contact the American Kennel Club and the national parent club, the Pug Dog Club of America (www.pugs.org) to be put in touch with respected and experienced people in the breed. In any case, you still need to be sure that the breeder's standards of care are what you would expect. You must also be as certain as you can be that the breeder fully understands his breed and has given careful consideration to the way the Pug has been bred, taking into consideration each dog's pedigree, health and overall soundness.

The breeder you select may be someone who breeds from home, in which case the puppies will hopefully have been brought up in the house and will be familiar with all the activities and noises of the family's daily routine. However, the breeder may run a larger establishment, in which the litter has perhaps been raised in a kennel situation. Still, if you have chosen your breeder wisely, the puppies will have had lots of contact and exposure to various people, sights and sounds. Even some of the larger breeding establishments whelp litters inside the home. In my personal opinion, this is infinitely better than the puppies' being raised entirely in a kennel environment, especially for small breeds such as the Pug.

However large or small the breeding establishment, it is important that the conditions in which the puppies are raised are

puppies full of fun with plenty of confidence.

The breeder should be perfectly willing to show you the dam. It will be interesting for you to take careful note of the mom's

Color in the Pug is purely a matter of personal preference. Black is less common than fawn, so be prepared for a longer wait if you have your heart set on a black puppy.

admirable. The areas should be clean and the puppies should be well supervised in a suitable environment. All should look in tip-top condition, and temperaments should be sound, the

temperament and how she interacts with her offspring. If the dam is not available for you to see, be warned that this might be a sign that the litter was not born on the premises, but has been brought in to be sold by a third party. This is far from ideal and not a situation in which you should consider buying a puppy.

As for the stud dog, it is likely that he will not be available, for he likely may be owned by someone else. A careful breeder may have traveled hundreds of miles to use this particular dog's stud services. Nonetheless, dedicated breeders will be able to show you at least a picture of him, as well as showing you his pedigree and telling you about him.

A well-chosen breeder will be able to give the new puppy owner lots of useful guidance, including advice about feeding. Some breeders give a small quantity of puppy food to each new owner when the puppies leave for new homes. In any event, the breeder should always provide written details of exactly what type and quantity of food has been fed, and with what regularity. You will, of course, be able to change the puppy's food and feeding schedule as time

Caring for a litter is hard work for a loving mom. Pups get the healthiest start in life by nursing from their dam.

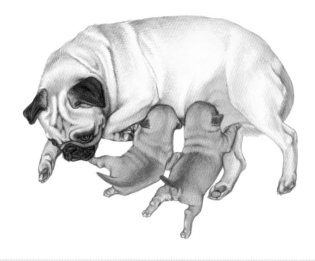

goes on, but any changes must be made gradually.

A breeder will tell you what vaccinations the puppy has received, if any, and any relevant documentation should be passed over at the time of purchase. Documentation includes the pedigree, registration papers, health guarantee, copies of the parents' health clearances, the pup's vaccination and worming records and a sales contract if the breeder has one. Many breeders provide temporary insurance coverage for their puppies. This is a good idea, and the new owner can subsequently decide whether or not to continue with this protection. As veterinary insurance is becoming more and more popular, and thus more widely accepted, it may be a beneficial option for you and your Pug.

SELECTING A PUG BREEDER

Overview

- Finding a Pug breeder will not be difficult, but taking the time to distinguish the reputable from the less-than-ethical will require research and effort.
- Start with the American Kennel Club and Pug Dog Club of America as your sources for breeder referrals.
- The breeder you select should fully understand the Pug and his special requirements, carefully planning each breeding for the betterment of the breed.
- The breeder's facilities should be clean and well maintained, providing the pups with ample opportunity for human contact.
- The breeder must be honest in discussing the pros and cons of the Pug and have all of the necessary documentation available for you.

Finding the Right Puppy

You probably think that if you go to visit a litter of Pug puppies you will fall for their considerable charms and will automatically come home with a cuddly puppy in your arms. Though you are almost certain to fall in love at first sight, you must be sensible in your approach. Do not allow your heart to rule your head. Not all breeders are reputable ones and not every Pug puppy is of good quality.

Be prepared to lose your heart with just one glance! It's tough to keep your wits about you when dealing with the absolutely irresistible Pug.

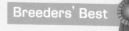

A healthy puppy should strike you as being clean, without any sign of discharge from the eyes or nose. His rear end should be spotless, with no sign of loose bowels. Although any puppy's nails can be sharp, they should not be too long. It should be

Peekaboo! Breeders allow visitors to the litter before the pups are ready to leave, so you can pick out your puppy and then return to bring him home at the appropriate time.

evident that the breeder has clipped the pup's nails as necessary.

The coat should clearly be in excellent condition, not tacky or sparse in any way, and there should be absolutely no signs of parasites. Parasites such as fleas and lice cannot always be easily seen, but will be indicated by the puppy's scratching. You might also notice a rash. Scratching, though, does not always mean that there is a parasitic or faulty skin condition, for it can also be associated with teething. In that

At only a few days old, these pups' eyes aren't even open yet! The breeder has a huge responsibility to care for these tiny pups.

case, the puppy will only scratch around his head area. When the second set of teeth have come through so that the gums are no longer sore, this scratching will stop.

Scratching might also be connected with an ear infection, so a quick look inside your potential puppy's ears will ensure that there is no build-up of wax. There also should be no odor from the ear. Of course, a good breeder will have checked that each puppy is in all-around good health before offering him for sale.

Screening requirements for genetic diseases may vary from country to country and breed to breed. Regardless, before purchasing your Pug, you should have checked with the Pug Dog Club of America or the AKC as to which tests for hereditary problems are expected to have been carried out on the parents of the litter and the pups themselves. You must ask the breeder to show you written proof of the results. Remember to take note of the test dates.

Most puppies are outgoing and full of fun, so do not take pity on the overly shy one that hides away in a corner. Your puppy should clearly enjoy your company when you come for a visit. This will make for a long-term bond between you. When you go to select your puppy, take with you the members of your immediate family with whom the puppy will spend time at home. It is essential that everyone in the family agrees with the important decision you are about to make, for a new puppy will inevitably change your lives.

The breeder should be honest in discussing any differences in puppy personalities. Although most breeders do some type of temperament testing, they also have spent most of their time over the past weeks cuddling and cleaning up after these

Tell the breeder if you plan to show your pup in conformation or participate in other areas of competition. Some pups will show more promise than others,

If you hope that your Pug will be a star in the show ring like this winning representative of the breed, the breeder will guide you to the pup with the most promise.

pups. By this point in time, they should know the subtle differences in each pup's personality. The breeder's observations are valuable aids in selecting a puppy that will be compatible with you and your lifestyle.

and he can help you select one that will best suit your long-term goals.

Do you prefer a male or a female? Which one is right for you? Both sexes are loving and loyal, and the differences are due to individual personalities more than sex. The Pug female is a gentle soul and easy to live with, but females can be a bit more moody or frivolous, depending on their whims and hormonal peaks.

Hopefully you will already have done plenty of research about the breed long before reaching the stage of having a new puppy enter your life. Keep this book on your shelf for permanent ease of reference, and you should

Observe the entire litter and watch them interact with each other. They should all be healthy and sound and kept in a clean, cozy area.

consider some other books on the breed so that you have a library of helpful Pug information handy.

Breed clubs are also important sources of help and information. Some even publish their own leaflets and small booklets about the breed, and might even publish a book of champions so that you can look back to see what your puppy's famous ancestors actually looked like. Most countries also have weekly or monthly canine newspapers or magazines, though you may have to order subscriptions, as these specialty publications are not always easily available at the local newstand.

Of course, those who have access to the Internet might also decide to look up breed information there. However, I would urge you not to take all you find online as truth. These days, anyone can set up a website and can write what they like, even though they may not have a sufficiently firm knowledge of the breed. Check out the AKC's and Pug Dog Club of America's websites, and follow links to regional club and member breeder sites to find trusted information from reputable Pug people.

Finally, it is a good idea to become a member of at least one breed club. In doing so, you will receive notification of breed-specific events in which you

Puppies mean papers, and we're not talking about their pedigrees. Have a house-breaking plan in mind before bringing your pup home. Clean living is essential to a happy relationship!

may like to participate, thus providing further opportunities to learn about the Pug and meet interesting people who share your love of the breed.

FINDING THE RIGHT PUPPY

Overview

- It's sure to be love at first sight with every Pug puppy that you see, but you must use your head to make a wise decision.
- Only consider a puppy from a healthy litter, sound in body and mind. Know which "red flags" warrant continuing your search elsewhere.
- What type of personality? Male or female? Pet or show? Know what type of Pug you are looking for and take the breeder's advice in finding a pup that suits you.
- Research, research, research! Before you visit any Pug puppies, be fully armed with knowledge of the breed and what to look for in a good breeder and puppy.

Welcoming the Pug

The great day on which your Pug puppy is to join you in your home will be the cause of much anticipation and excitement, but there will also be a lot of planning to do. You will have to consider many things, such as where the puppy is to sleep, what he is going to eat, the equipment he will need and, not least, the safety of your home and the security of the fencing around your yard. Soon you will be able to collect your Pug to bring home. For this momentous day,

Be ready for your new addition! Have all of the essentials for your puppy before he comes home.

you will want to be certain that every-thing at home is prepared as thoroughly as it can possibly be.

Hopefully, during your visits to the litter you will have had the opportunity to select your puppy before the date of collection. Should this be the case, you will have had plenty of chance to discuss with the breeder exactly what your puppy will need to make his life healthy, safe and also enjoyable.

Welcoming a Pug into your home means looking forward to years ahead of joyful companionship with a delightful canine friend.

Depending on where you live, you will probably have easy access to a good pet-supply store, whether one of the large outlets or a good privately owned shop. If you can find a shop that is owned by people who show their own dogs, they should have a wide range of items and will probably be able to give sensible guidance as to what you need to buy. Major dog shows also usually have a large display of trade stands that cater to a dog's every need and whim.

The earlier you begin grooming your Pug, the better accustomed he will be to the routine and the better behaved he will be for his beauty sessions. Have all of the necessary equipment on hand.

You will certainly need some grooming equipment for your Pug puppy, albeit basic. At this early age, a gentle brush and a grooming glove will be your principal needs. Some owners also like to use a fine-toothed steel comb. You will also need canine nail clippers. Certain things, like cotton balls and towels, you probably already have in stock as household items. If you choose to dry your dog's coat with a dryer, you will be able to make do with your own hair dryer on the lowest heat setting instead of investing in one of the special canine dryers.

Where your puppy is to sleep will be a major consideration, and you should start with a crate. It is only natural that the newcomer will be restless for the first couple of nights or so, but if you immediately take pity on the little soul and let him join you in your bedroom, he will expect to remain there always! Hence, it is essential that the bedding you choose should be suitable so that your puppy can rest as comfortably as possible in the

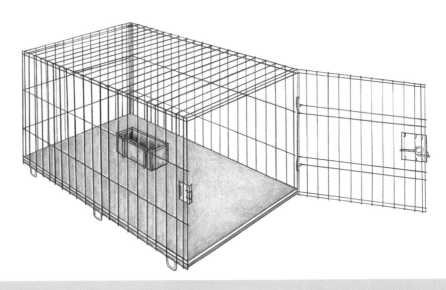

Your Pug's crate will become his home within a home. The wire crate is good for use indoors, as it gives the dog a clear view of his surroundings and allows him to feel part of what's going on.

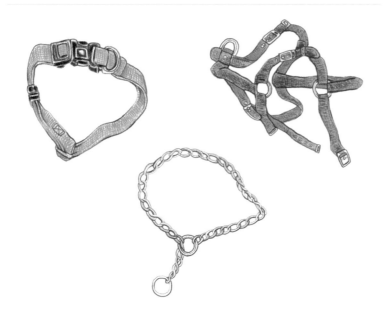

Three choices for collars. Clockwise from upper right: halter, chain choke collar and traditional buckle collar.

intended place. Soft padding and/or blankets in his crate will serve his needs nicely.

Assuming that your Pug is to live inside your home, as he must, rather than outdoors or in a kennel, the choice of his crate and bedding acces-sories is very much a matter of personal preference. With a small breed like the Pug, your puppy will not be overwhelmed in an adult-sized crate, so you should purchase a crate from the outset that will comfortably

Once your Pug is reliably heel-trained, the retractable lead is a good option. The lead expands to give the dog a wider range to explore, and it easily retracts when you need to keep him close.

house your Pug at his full size. However, bearing in mind that a puppy will not want a crate that is too large, and that a too-large crate will be ineffective for house-breaking, you may have to partition the crate or put in

them, and sharp wicker pieces can all too easily injure eyes or break off and be swallowed. It is wiser to choose a durable crate that can be washed or wiped down. The padding or bedding that you choose must

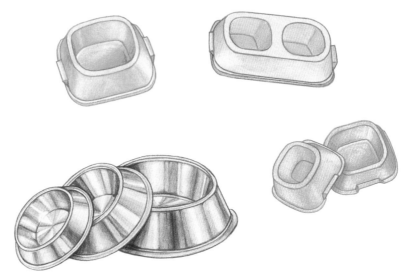

Select sturdy bowls for your Pug, made of hard plastic or stainless steel.

additional bedding to create a smaller living area with a cozy atmosphere. These things can be taken away as the Pug grows to give him more room.

Wicker beds may look pretty, but they are dangerous because puppies like to chew

also be able to be washed frequently, for it will be important that all your dog's bedding is kept clean and dry.

Although a Pug is small, he can get into all kinds of mischief. Everyday household items may seem harmless enough, but a dainty cloth draped over the side of a little table full of fragile ornaments is merely asking for trouble! Even more dangerous to a mischievous puppy are electrical cords, so be sure they are put well beyond his reach. Tiny teeth can bite

poisonous, so please keep them out of the way of temptation. Antifreeze is especially dangerous to dogs, as animals are attracted to its taste, and it can kill a dog, large or small, with just a few drops.

Puppies will explore anything they can get their noses into! Keep this in mind when creating a dog-proof environment for your Pug.

through an electrical cord all too easily, causing what can be a fatal accident. Another word of warning concerns cleaning agents, gardening aids and all other household chemicals. Many of these contain substances that are

When your puppy first arrives home, it is only natural that you will be proud. You will want to show your new-found companion to your friends. However, your puppy is making a big move in his short life, so the first

CHAPTER 6

Be aware of hidden doggie hazards around the home and yard. For example, gardening chemicals, fertilizers and mulch contain substances toxic to dogs, so keep your Pug's environment free of these dangers.

two or three days are best spent quietly at home with you and your immediate family. Once your puppy has taken stock of his new surroundings, you will be able to introduce him to lots of new people. If you have young children, or if they visit, always carefully supervise any time spent with your young puppy. Youngsters can all too easily hurt a small puppy, even with the best of intentions.

If your family has other pets, introductions should be made slowly and under close supervision. Most Pugs get along well with other animals, but you should always exercise caution until you are certain that all concerned are going to be the best of friends.

Additionally, your pup must receive certain vaccinations before it is safe for him to be around other animals, as he will be vulnerable to illness. Ask your vet when it will be safe to introduce your Pug to new canine friends.

WELCOMING THE PUG

Overview

- Before your puppy comes home, you should be prepared with all of the necessary accessories like a leash, a collar, puppy food, food and water bowls, grooming equipment and the like.
- Prepare a safe and comfortable place for your Pug to sleep. He will need a suitable dog crate and padding, and perhaps a dog bed.
- Puppy-proof your home by removing all potential dangers, both indoors and out.
- Make your Pug's introductions to the family low-key, being especially careful when introducing your pup to children and/or other pets.

Pug Puppy Kindergarten

When your Pug puppy first arrives at your home, everything will be new to him. Although he is usually full of confidence, it may take him a little while to feel completely at ease in his new surroundings. It is essential that you appreciate this, recognizing that there will be no familiar sights, sounds or smells to make him feel at home. Now that he is living with you, it is you who must provide him with the confidence and encouragement he needs throughout his new learning experiences.

A well-adjusted Pug is a happy, confident member of the family with whom it is a pleasure to share your life and home.

When your puppy first comes home, you should begin by getting him used to all family members who live there. Instilling confidence in your Pug will help with his early socialization, and you will soon be able to introduce him to your wider family and your friends. Please try not to bombard him with too many new people and situations all at the same time, though.

Depending on the age of your puppy, and whether his course of vaccinations is complete, you may or may not be able to take him out in public places immediately. Whichever the case, I would still advise you to allow him to settle down at home for the first few days before venturing further. There will be lots you can do with your Pug puppy at home, so you will both undoubtedly have great fun together. Puppies tire easily, though, so allow him to get sufficient rest, too.

Don't bombard your Pug with too many new friends all at the same time, and make sure that children know how to handle him properly.

Although not especially well known for his retrieving skills, your Pug will enjoy a flying disk to play with outdoors.

If restricted to your home territory for a little while, you can play games with your puppy, with suitably safe, soft toys, but do not allow him to tug on anything too strongly. Check regularly that sharp or unsafe parts, such as plastic "squeakers," do not become detached from the toy, as they can cause injury. Your puppy's teeth will be very sharp, so toys can easily be damaged.

Whether or not you plan to show your Pug, it is always good to do a little early training, getting him to stand calmly on a table and to lie on his side to be gently groomed. This training will be helpful on numerous occasions, including visits to the vet. It is much easier to deal with a well-behaved dog in situations like this, and you will be so proud of your clever companion!

Accustom your puppy to being on a lead, which is always a strange experience for a tiny youngster. Begin by just putting a simple buckle collar on him. The collar should not be too tight, nor should it be so loose that it can be caught

Decide on the house rules and enforce them consistently, starting right away. For example, don't allow your Pug on the sofa today and then scold him for jumping up to sit next to you tomorrow.

on things, causing panic and possible injury. Just put the collar on the pup for a few minutes at a time, lengthening each time period slightly until your puppy feels comfortable in his first item of "clothing." Don't expect miracles; this may take a few days.

When he is comfortable in the collar, attach a small, lightweight lead. The lead you select must have a secure catch, yet be simple to attach and release as necessary. Until now, your puppy has simply gone where he has pleased and he will find it very strange to be attached to someone who is restricting his movements. For this reason, when training my own

puppies, I like to allow them to "take" me for the first few sessions, after which I begin to exert a little pressure,

After your Pug is accustomed to being walked on a leash, you may want to switch to using a nylon harness, as this is thought by some owners to be more comfortable for the dog.

guiding the pup in the direction that I want to walk. Soon enough, training can start in earnest, with the puppy coming with me as I lead the way.

Chapter 7

The sit command is an easy command for most dogs to learn and the first step on the road to your Pug's knowledge of the basic commands.

It is usual to begin training the puppy to walk on your left-hand side. When this has been accomplished to your satisfaction, you can try moving him on your right, but there is absolutely no hurry. If you plan to show your Pug, you will generally move your dog on your left, but there are occasions when it is necessary also to move him on your right so as not to obstruct the judge's view.

As your puppy gets older, you can teach him to sit. Always use a simple one-word command, such as "Sit," while exerting gentle pressure on his rump to show him what you expect. This will take a little time, but you will soon succeed. Always remember to give your pup plenty of praise when he performs the exercise. Never shout or get angry when your dog does not achieve your aim, for this will do more harm than

good. If yours is destined to be a show dog, you may decide not to teach "sit," as in the show ring he will be expected to stand. One

Some Pugs just can't contain their joy at the sight of their crates, their very own special places!

option is to teach him to sit, but not sit/stay, teaching the stand/stay instead.

When your Pug puppy can venture into public places, begin by taking him somewhere quiet, without too many distractions. Soon you will find his confidence increasing and you can then introduce him to new places with exciting sights, sounds and smells. He must always be on a safe lead that cannot be slipped (quite different from the type used in the show ring). When you have total confidence in one another, you will probably be able to let him off-lead, but always keep him in sight, and be sure the place you have chosen for free exercise is com-

pletely safe and securely fenced in.

Whether you have a potential show dog or your Pug is purely to be a companion, you will need to train your puppy to stay in a crate when required. At shows in most countries, toy breeds are housed in crates for at least part of the time while not being actually exhibited in the ring. Crates are useful for safe traveling and, if used in the home,

Accustoming your Pug to standing still on a table has advantages, as he will learn to stand politely for grooming sessions and for evaluation by the judge if you plan to show.

most dogs seem to look upon their crates as safe places to go and don't mind staying in them. The crate also is an invaluable tool in housebreaking, as the pup will not want to soil his special place and will thus learn to "hold it" until he is let out to relieve himself.

When you commence crate training, put your pup into his crate and remain within his sight. Give him a toy or treat to occupy his mind and to help him associate the crate with good things. To begin, leave him in the crate for very short spells of just a minute or two, then gradually build up the timespan.

It should not take your Pug long to get used to his crate, and you will be pleased with the results of your efforts. The crate will benefit you and your Pug in so many circumstances that the time you take to accustom your Pug to his crate will be well worth it. It's an essential tool for training and, most importantly, for your dog's safety.

PUG PUPPY KINDERGARTEN

Overview

- It will take your Pug a few days to feel comfortable in his new surroundings. Be attentive and affectionate, careful not to overwhelm him with too much too soon.
- Have fun with your puppy by engaging him in games with his toys.
- Introduce your pup to his collar and lead. This is a precursor to any type of training.
- Always ensure your Pug's safety when out in public places.
- Learn the many benefits of a dog crate and the correct way to use it for your Pug's training and safety.

House-training Your Pug

When your darling Pug puppy looks up at you with those glorious eyes of his, you will ask yourself whether you will ever have the heart to discipline him. He will have to be trained and, although you must be kind, you must never allow him to get away with too much, no matter how sweetly he looks at you. Remember that this is an intelligent little breed, and it will not be beyond your Pug's brain capacity to figure out exactly how to get the better of you! To house-train

Controlling where your dog can and cannot go is an important part of teaching your Pug the rules of the house and keeping him safe, both indoors and outdoors.

with success, you will need to be consistent and firm, but never harsh, and you must certainly never be rough with your Pug.

When your puppy first comes into your home, he may or may not already be house-trained, albeit to a limited extent. Regardless, you must always realize that your home is completely different from the breeder's, so he will have to relearn the house rules. Doors will not be located in the same places and your family may go to bed and rise at different times. It will undoubtedly take him a little time to learn and to adapt.

The speed of your house-training success will depend to a certain extent on your own environment, your family's routine and the season of the year. Most puppies are perfectly happy to go out to relieve themselves in dry weather but, when it is cold or raining, many feel rather

After using his toilet area just once, a dog will be able to use his sense of smell to locate it. This is the basis of training him always to go to the same spot to do his business.

If you allow your Pug free run of the house, you may be surprised at where he will turn up. This is a small dog and, thus, can fit into many little hiding places.

differently and will need more encouragement!

Paper training is always useful in the very early stages of training. The paper should be placed by the door so that the dog learns to associate the paper with the exit to the wide world outside. When he uses the paper, he should be praised. Obviously, it is ideal if the puppy can be let out as soon as he shows any sign of wanting to relieve himself. Again, this may depend on whether your home has immediate access to a fenced yard and whether or not the pup's course of vaccinations is complete. For those without a fenced yard you will need to get into a routine of taking your Pug out on his lead for bathroom visits.

Remember that puppies need to go to the toilet much more frequently than adult animals, certainly immediately after waking

and following meals. In fact, to take your pup outside every hour while he is awake is not a bad idea at all. Always keep your eyes and ears open, for a youngster will not be able to wait those extra two or three minutes until it is convenient for you to let him out. If you delay, accidents will certainly happen, so be warned!

As your puppy matures, his "asking" to be let out when necessary will become second nature. It will be very rare if you have a Pug that is unclean in the house. A stud dog, however, can be different, for he may well want to mark his territory, and your table and chair legs may be just the places that he chooses!

Simple commands are very helpful, "Potty" and "Let's go" being common, and they seem to work. Never, *ever* forget to give praise when the deed is done in the desired place. However, if a potty accident happens indoors, you should give your pup a verbal reprimand. It is essential to keep in mind that scolding for accidents or any other misbehavior will work only if your Pug is *caught in the act*. If you try to reprimand him after the fact, he will simply not know what he has done wrong, which will only

House-training is the first lesson you will attempt with your puppy. It is the key to your clean and happy life together.

Ready to go! If you are consistent in establishing and sticking to a schedule, your Pug will learn what his potty trips are for, and he will wait for these trips outdoors to relieve himself.

serve to confuse him.

It is essential that any accidents are cleaned up immediately. If a dog has done his toilet in the wrong place, the mess must be cleaned thoroughly so as to disguise the smell. If the dog smells it, he may want to use that particular place again. When your puppy is old enough to be exercised in public places, always carry with you a "poop-scoop" or small plastic bag so that any droppings can be removed. The anti-dog

The toileting behavior of males has a dual purpose; the first, obviously, is to relieve themselves, while the second is to mark territory with their "calling cards."

lobby exists everywhere, so please give them no cause for complaint; additionaly, "poop-scoop" laws are enforced in most every city and town.

HOUSE-TRAINING YOUR PUG

Overview

- The first type of training you will attempt with your Pug is house-training, teaching him proper toileting habits.
- Your success in house-training depends on your diligence in taking the puppy out and establishing a schedule.
- Know at what times your pup will need to go out and learn to recognize the signs he gives you.
- Only reprimand for an accident if you "catch him in the act." Otherwise, he will have no idea why you are scolding him, thus serving no purpose while creating fear and confusion in the pup.
- Be a responsible dog owner and always pick up after your dog.

Teaching Basic Commands

T he Pug is renowned for his charm, dignity and intelligence. The latter makes him perfectly capable of being trained, but sometimes his charm and dignity get in the way! A Pug likes to know why he is expected to do something and may decide not to carry out your instructions to the letter without having reasoned things out in his brain. You must always be gentle and consistent in your approach. It is not a good idea to try to force a Pug to do something that

Before getting started with the basic commands, the Pug must be accustomed to his everyday collar and lead.

he feels would be better suited to "lesser mortals."

Although some show dogs are trained in obedience, many exhibitors feel this can be detrimental to a dog's performance in the show ring. This you will have to bear in mind from the outset if you plan to show, but all dogs must learn the basics for good manners and safety. Therefore, how you approach teaching commands may differ according to whether you have a show or pet-only dog.

In all training, it is essential to get your dog's full attention, which many owners do with the aid of treats. The dog learns to associate treats with praise and learns to associate these rewards with doing things correctly (positive reinforcement). The following training method involves using food treats, although you will wean your dog off these training aids in time so that your reward system is eventually based on mostly praise

Dogs must demonstrate their knowledge of the heel command in the show ring for the judge's evaluation of their movement. Of course, heeling is necessary for show and pet dogs alike.

A closer look at a "well-heeled" Pug on the move.

with an occasional treat. (Remember the Pug's tendency to become overweight!). Always use very simple commands, just one or two short words. Keep sessions short so that they do not become boring for your dog. Dogs, especially intelligent ones, will easily tire of repetition.

SIT

With the lead in your left hand, hold a small treat in your right, letting your dog smell or lick the treat, but not yet taking it. Move the treat away as you say "sit," your hand rising slowly over the dog's head so that he looks upward. In doing so, he will bend his knees and sit. When

Let your Pug know what you expect of him by gently guiding him into the sit while you issue the verbal command "Sit," rewarding him when he assumes the position.

Once your Pug is reliable in the sit, step out in front of him to teach the sit/stay, keeping him on lead at first and practicing in a secure, distraction-free area.

this has been accomplished, give him his treat and lavish praise.

HEEL

A dog trained to walk to heel will walk alongside his handler without pulling. Again the lead should be held in your left hand while the dog assumes the sit position next to your left leg. Hold the end of the lead in your right

command him to sit again. Repeat this procedure until he carries out the task of walking three steps without pulling. Then you can increase the number of strides to five, seven and so on. Give verbal praise and a treat at the close of each section of the exercise. At the end of the session, let him enjoy himself with a free run in the fenced yard.

This Pug is practicing the down exercise with a patient handler and a tasty treat.

hand, but also control it lower down with your left.

Step forward with your right foot, saying the word "heel." To begin, just take three steps and then

DOWN

When your dog is proficient in sitting, you can introduce the word "down." It is essential to first understand that a dog will consider the down position as a submissive one, and thus won't be so eager to assume the down position, so gentle training is important.

With your Pug sitting by talking gently. He will follow the treat, lowering himself down. When his elbows touch the floor, you can release the treat and give him praise, but try to get him to remain there

When teaching the stay in either the sit or down, use your hand as a "stop sign" along with your verbal command "Stay."

your left leg, as for the sit, hold the lead in your left hand and a treat in your right. Place your left hand on top of the dog's shoulders (without pushing) and hold the treat under his nose, saying "down" in a quiet tone of voice. Gradually move the treat along the floor, in front of the dog, all the while

for a few seconds before getting up. Gradually the time of the down exercise can be increased.

STAY

The stay exercise can be taught with your dog in either a sit or in a down position, as usual with the lead in your left hand and the treat in your right. Allow him to lick the treat as you say "stay," while standing directly in front of the dog, having moved from your position beside him. Silently count to about five, then move back to your original position alongside him, allowing your dog to have the treat while giving him lavish praise.

Keep practicing "stay" just as described for a few days, then gradually increase the distance between you, using your hand with the palm facing the dog as an indication that he must stay where he is. Soon you should be able to do this exercise

When your Pug is enjoying some time off-lead, you need to be confident that he will respond when you call him to come to you.

without a lead in your securely enclosed training area, and your Pug will increasingly stay for longer periods of time. Always give lavish praise and a treat upon completion of the exercise.

COME
Your Pug will love to come back to you when called. The idea is to invite him to return, offering a treat and giving lots of praise when he does so. It is important to teach the "come" command, also known as the "recall," for this should bring your dog running back to you if ever he is in danger of moving out of sight.

Always take special care *never* to call your dog when across a road on which traffic is passing. This could be enormously dangerous. It is also very important to remember that you must *never* call your dog to come to you for punishment. If you do, he will quickly learn that coming to you results in his getting yelled at or scolded, so he will learn to run the other way when you call. Always reinforce his coming to you with praise, petting and an occasional treat so that he will look forward to answering your call and will do so reliably.

TRICKS

The Pug is truly a charming little character and may well enjoy learning a fun trick or two. What you teach, if anything at all, will be very much a matter of choice, but some dogs learn to offer their paws and others like to sit up and "beg," which is particularly enchanting.

KEEP PRACTICING

Ongoing practice in obedience is actually a lifetime dog rule. Dogs will be dogs and, if we don't maintain their skills, they will sink back into sloppy, inattentive behaviors that will be harder to correct. Incorporate these commands into your daily routine and your dog will remain a gentleman or lady of whom you can be proud.

TEACHING BASIC COMMANDS

Overview

- Lessons in basic obedience ensure that your Pug will grow up into a polite, well-mannered dog.
- Keep training sessions interesting and not too long so that your Pug doesn't become bored and lose focus on the lesson.
- Treats are helpful as both attention-getters and rewards in training.
- The basic commands include sit, heel, down, stay and come. For some fun with your clownish Pug, you can throw in a few tricks, too!
- Keep practicing. Find ways to incorporate the commands into your everyday routine.

Home Care for Your Pug

Your Pug is undoubtedly precious to you, so you will want to do all in your power to keep him in good health throughout his life, which you hope will be a long one. Routine care on a daily basis is very important, for this will maintain your dog in good condition and help you to catch and treat any problems early on. You will get to know your Pug well and thus be able to recognize if he's not acting like his normal self. This will help you to see problems arising so

Your Pug is a true family member and you want the longest life possible for him. It goes without saying that you'll give him the best of care.

that you can take your pet to the vet without delay for further investigation.

DENTAL CARE

Keeping teeth in good condition is your responsibility. You owe this to your dog, for dental problems do not just stop inside the mouth. When gums are infected, all sorts of heath problems can subsequently arise, with the infection spreading through the system and possibly leading even to consequent death.

Home care means keeping your Pug out of harm's way. Baby gates in the home are helpful for keeping dogs within the safe dog-proof areas in the home.

You may clean the teeth of your Pug extremely gently and carefully, using a very small toothbrush and special canine toothpaste, not toothpaste made for humans. Take particular care if any of the puppy teeth are beginning to loosen. Your dog may not like this procedure much at first, but should easily get used to it if you clean his teeth regularly. Experienced breeders

Chew toys with raised knobs have dental benefits in that the knobs act as plaque removers as the dog chews.

sometimes use a special dental scraper, although this is not recommended for the novice.

When cleaning the teeth, always check the gums for signs of inflammation. If you notice that the gums look red or swollen, a visit to your vet is advised.

FIRST AID

Accidents can happen and, if they do, you must remain as cool, calm and collected as possible under the circumstances. You should acquaint yourself with emergency situations and their symptoms, as well as first-aid techniques. You want to be able to help your Pug as quickly as possible while contacting the vet and awaiting further advice. Check and see if your breed club or local humane society offers canine first-aid seminars, which are helpful and informative for dog owners.

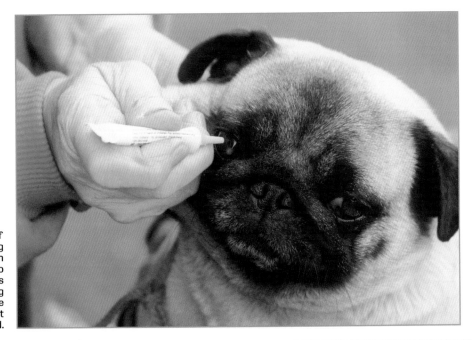

Be careful of the Pug's big eyes, which are prone to injury. This Pug is having some eye ointment applied.

Insect stings are quite common. If it is still there, the "stinger" should be removed with tweezers. Ice can be applied to reduce the swelling, and an accurate dosage of antihistamine treatment (ask your vet) can be given. If a sting is inside the dog's mouth, consult your vet at once.

Accidental poisoning is also a worry, as dogs can investigate all sorts of things, not all of which are safe. If you suspect poisoning, try to ascertain the cause, because treatment may vary according to the type of poison ingested. Vomiting or sudden bleeding from an exit point, such as the gums, can be an indication of poisoning. Immediate veterinary attention is essential.

Small abrasions should be cleansed thoroughly and antiseptic applied. In the case of serious bleeding,

initially apply pressure above the area. For minor burns, apply cool water.

In the case of shock, such as following a car accident, keep the dog

Take special care of your Pug in his senior years. It is especially important not to let the older dog put on excess weight.

warm while veterinary aid is sought right away.

For heat stroke, cold water must be applied immediately, especially over the dogs's shoulders. In severe cases, the dog should be submerged in water up to his neck if possible. Dogs can die quickly from heat stroke, so fast veterinary attention is of paramount importance. Conversely, in the case of hypothermia, keep the dog warm with hot-water bottles and give a warm bath if possible while contacting the vet.

RECOGNIZING HEALTH SIGNS

If you love your Pug and you spend plenty of time together, you will know when something is amiss. He may "go off" his food or seem dull and listless. His eyes, usually bright and alive, may seem to have lost their sparkle, and his coat may look dull rather than healthy and shiny.

Changes in toileting may also be indicative of ill health. Loose bowels usually clear up within 24 hours, but if they go on for longer than this, especially if you see blood, you will need to visit your vet.

Also keep a lookout for increased thirst and an increase in the frequency of urination. These signs could indicate any of a number of problems.

CHECKING FOR PARASITES

It is essential to keep your dog's coat in top condition or parasites may take hold, causing the health of the skin and coat to deteriorate. It is often not easy to see parasites. If you catch sight of even one flea, you can be sure there will be more lurking somewhere. There are now several good preventative aids available for external parasites, and your vet will be able to advise you about which ones are safest and most effective, for in some areas the best remedies are not available in shops.

Dogs, just like humans, run the risk of insect bites, bee stings and the like when spending time outdoors. Check your Pug's skin and coat regularly for any signs of such problems.

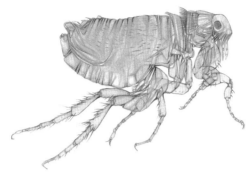

An enlarged view of a flea, an enemy that most every dog owner will fight at some point in his dog's life.

Also be on the continual lookout for ear mites. These cannot be seen, but a brown discharge with some odor from the ear is a clear indication that they are present. A suitable ear treatment will be available from your vet.

A dog can also carry internal parasites in the form of various types of worms. Roundworms are the most common and tapeworms, although less frequent, can be even more debilitating.

Heartworms are transmitted by mosquitoes and presently seem only to be

A healthy, happy trio! Dogs can transmit illnesses to other dogs, so be sure that the dogs with which your Pug spends time are in good health.

present in dogs in America, Asia, Australia and Central Europe. However, with the increasing passage of dogs from one country to another, we should all be aware that heartworms exist, for they can be very dangerous. Your veterinarian will advise you if a preventative regimen is necessary and, if so, ask him to recommend the safest way to protect your dog.

Routine worming and testing for worms are

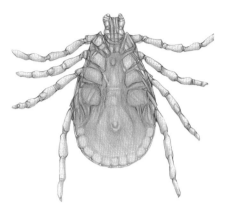

A close-up look at a tick, an external parasite that can transmit serious diseases to animals and humans.

essential throughout a dog's life. Of course, veterinary recommendation as to a suitable parasite-control regimen is necessary.

HOME CARE FOR YOUR PUG

Overview

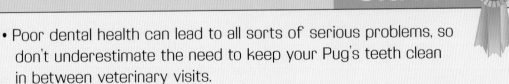

- Poor dental health can lead to all sorts of serious problems, so don't underestimate the need to keep your Pug's teeth clean in between veterinary visits.
- Acquaint yourself with the signs of health problems and emergencies, and learn basic canine first-aid techniques.
- If you know your Pug well, you will easily be able to recognize changes in his behavior that indicate something is wrong.
- Dogs can fall victim to many types of common parasites. Be sure that your Pug is protected and check his skin and coat regularly. Checks for internal parasites can be done by the vet.

Feeding Your Pug

The majority of Pugs thoroughly enjoy their food, which can often lead to problems of obesity. Keep this in mind from the very outset. An overweight dog is likely to encounter more health problems than one kept at the correct weight for his breed. Obesity puts strain on the heart as well as on the joints, and can lead to increased risk under anesthesia.

Today there is an enormous range of specially prepared foods available for dogs. Many of them are

The breeder starts the pups off on solid food as part of the weaning process.

scientifically balanced and formulated for specific sizes of dog and age ranges. Because the Pug is only a small breed, if you feed dry foods it is probably sensible to select those described by the manufacturer as "small bite" size.

The type of food, amounts fed and meal schedule will change as your puppy matures. The breeder's experience with the Pug will help you plan your dog's diet at all stages of life.

It is really a matter of personal preference as to which dog food you decide to use, though initially your choice will be influenced by the type of food that has been fed to your new puppy by his breeder. Changes can, of course, be made to the pup's diet, but never change suddenly from one food to another or your Pug is likely to get an upset tummy.

If making a change, introduce the new brand of food gradually over a few days until the old brand is phased out. There is usually no harm at all in changing the flavor of food while keeping with the same brand.

You'll appreciate the value of treats for motivating and rewarding your Pug in training, but don't overdo it! Try to resist your Pug's pleading eyes, as an overweight dog is more prone to health problems.

Should you decide to feed a dry food, make sure that you thoroughly read the feeding instructions. Some dry foods need to be moistened, especially those for young-sters. Dry food should also be stored carefully, bearing in mind that its vitamin value declines if not used fairly quickly, usually within about three months. It is essential that a plentiful supply of fresh water is available for your dog, especially when feeding dry food. Regardless of the type of food, dogs should have access to drinking water at all times.

Because of the enormous range of products available, you may find it difficult to make a choice without advice from your vet, your breeder or another Pug enthusiast. However, keep in mind that in adulthood an active dog will require a higher protein content than one that lives a sedentary life.

No dog should ever be fed the type of chocolate products that humans eat, as this is carcinogenic to dogs. In fact, more attention is being paid to "people foods" that are toxic to dogs; aside from chocolate, these include onions, certain types of nut, grapes and raisins. As a rule, Pug owners should avoid feeding their dogs from their own plates in any case, as Pugs won't turn down a tidbit and are prone to obesity.

Some owners prefer to feed fresh foods, preparing their dogs' meals themselves rather than using manufac-tured products. In this case, owners should be absolutely certain that they are feeding a well-balanced diet, and that no dangerous things like bones of any type are included in the meals.

Many owners are tempted to feed tidbits between meals. This is not a good idea, as weight can pile on a Pug almost imperceptibly. A very suitable alternative is to give the occasional piece of carrot.

Most dogs love them! Carrots don't put on any weight and are useful aids to keeping the dog's teeth clean.

How many times a day you feed your adult Pug will probably be a matter of preference and personal routine. Many people divide the daily portion into morning and evening meals, while others prefer to give just one meal, perhaps with a light snack at the other end of the day. Obviously, puppies need to be fed more frequently, but your dog's breeder will give you good advice in this regard, and the transition to one or two meals a day will be made gradually as the dog matures.

As a dog reaches his senior years, his metabolism changes. Thus, feeding requirements may also change, typically from one or two meals a day to smaller meals fed more frequently. By then you will have gotten to know your pet well and you should be able to adjust his feeding accordingly. If you have any queries, your vet will be able to guide you in the right direction.

FEEDING YOUR PUG

Overview

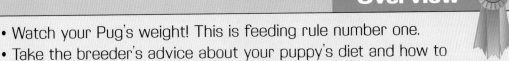

- Watch your Pug's weight! This is feeding rule number one.
- Take the breeder's advice about your puppy's diet and how to make changes as he grows up.
- Choose a high-quality food that provides balanced and complete nutrition for your Pug and is appropriate to his size, age and activity level.
- Don't give too many treats and avoid offering "people food" to your Pug altogether.
- Your Pug's dietary needs will change with different stages of life. This includes type of food, amount of food and feeding schedule.

Grooming Your Pug

Although your Pug has a short coat, his coat still needs to be cared for well if you wish to keep your dog in good condition and health. Just think of a human with short hair—his hair must still be kept clean and combed, or the person would look most unkempt!

Ideally your Pug will be groomed on a firm table with a non-slip surface. You will find that Pug owners choose their grooming equipment according to what they find suits them best. You will

Breeders often introduce their puppies to gentle grooming, making it a positive experience that they should grow to enjoy.

hopefully get good advice from the breeder about grooming when you discuss your new puppy's care. Once you become accustomed to grooming your Pug, you will develop your own preferences.

COAT CARE

However frequently you choose to bathe your Pug, it is essential to keep the coat clean and to groom him regularly. It is always wise to check the coat and wrinkles every day so that no unexpected problems start to build up under those folds of skin.

Part of your Pug's grooming routine is keeping his eyes (and surrounding areas), ears and facial wrinkles clean.

In a full grooming session, some people like to initially comb through with a fine-toothed steel comb or a grooming rake. This will help to remove any dead hair, and Pugs *do* shed! In doing this, you will also see if any dirt has accumulated on the coat, which will probably mean that it's time to bathe your Pug. On the other hand, some owners who groom

A grooming rake is helpful in ridding the coat of any dead hair. Pugs shed year round, so the more you groom, the less hair you'll find around the house.

regularly manage to do without a comb at all, just using a brush. The rake is especially helpful during times of heavy shedding, as it reaches all the way down to get rid of hair being shed. Remember, though, Pugs shed all year round!

Even if you have combed through, you will still need to use a soft bristle brush to go through the coat again. After this, you should use a grooming mitt (also called a hound glove), which will both groom the coat and massage the skin. Your Pug will enjoy a good massage! For the finishing touch, you will go over the coat with a chamois leather or a piece of velvet. There are grooming products available that fit on the hand, made of soft leather on one side and velvet on the other. These can be very useful with short-coated breeds.

It is of the utmost importance to take care of the Pug's facial wrinkles, which must never be allowed to get sore or infected. If there is any sign that something is amiss, the wrinkles must be wiped clean gently and smeared with lanolin or petroleum jelly. This is a precaution against infection. Should you have a black Pug, you may find that his wrinkles tend to become more greasy than usual, so take special care. Visit your vet if there are signs of infection. Along these lines, you must never allow your Pug's nose to become too dry.

BATHING YOUR PUG
Many Pug owners who exhibit their dogs like to bathe them prior to each show. This is usually necessary for blacks. Regular bathing is important to maintain healthy skin and a shiny coat. If a puppy is accustomed to being bathed from a young age, he will be perfectly happy to accept this part of the grooming

procedure as he grows older.

Always brush your Pug's coat thoroughly before

ears. It is usually wise to wash the head last so that shampoo does not drip into

Black Pugs may require a little extra attention to their grooming, such as more frequent bathing and extra care of the facial wrinkles, to keep the coat looking velvety and shiny.

bathing. Then stand your dog on a non-slip surface and test the water temperature on the back of your own hand. Use a canine shampoo, not a human one, taking care not to get water into the eyes and

the eyes while you are concentrating on another part of the body. Take care to reach all the slightly awkward places so that no area is neglected.

Rinse your Pug

thoroughly, as shampoo left in the coat can cause dryness and itchiness. Then, once he is rinsed, carefully lift your Pug out of the bath, wrapped in a warm, clean towel, and dry him with the aid of a hair dryer set on the lowest heat setting. Remember that many dogs do not like air blowing towards their faces, so guide the flow of air away from your Pug's face. Never allow your Pug to become cold when wet and do not let him outdoors until he is completely dry.

EARS AND EYES
It is important to keep your Pug's eyes and ears clean. They should be carefully

On a warm, sunny day, bathing outdoors can be fun for the Pug and the family.

wiped with a damp cloth or cotton ball, perhaps using a specially formulated product available from good pet stores. Special cleaning solutions are made for the ears and also for the eyes.

If your dog has been shaking his head or scratching at his ears, there may well be an infection or ear mites. A thick brown discharge and malodorous smell are also indicative of these problems, so veterinary consultation is needed immediately.

At any sign of injury to the eye, or if the eye turns blue, veterinary attention must be sought. If an eye injury is dealt with quickly, it often can be repaired, but if neglected, it can lead to loss of sight.

NAILS AND FEET

Nails must always be kept at the proper length, but how frequently they need clipping depends very much on the surface upon which your dog walks. Dogs living their lives primarily on carpets or on grass will need more frequent attention to their nails than those who regularly move on a hard surface.

Your Pug should be trained to accept nail clipping from an early age. Take great care not to cut into the quick, which is the blood vessel that runs through the nail, for this will be painful to him. It is a good idea to keep a styptic pencil or some styptic powder handy to stem the flow of blood in case of accident. Cutting just a small

Start with the basics for your Pug puppy, and add to your collection of equipment as you develop your own grooming preferences.

Pug

Dark nails can be challenging to clip, but walking on hard surfaces helps to keep a dog's nails worn down to a proper length.

sliver of nail at a time is the safest approach.

You should also inspect feet regularly to be sure that the pads have not become cracked and that nothing has become wedged or embedded between them. Even road tar can get stuck on the foot pads, and butter is useful for removing this should it happen.

Inspect your Pug's feet and clip his nails as needed; also be sure that there is no excess hair between the footpads or anything embedded in the pads.

ANAL GLANDS

A dog's anal glands are located on both sides of the anal opening. Sometimes these become blocked and require evacuation. Experienced breeders often do this themselves, but pet owners would be well advised to leave this to their vets, for damage can be caused if done incorrectly, and evacuation is not always necessary.

GROOMING YOUR PUG

Overview

- The Pug is not a high-maintenance breed when it comes to grooming, but special attention needs to be paid to keeping his wrinkles clean.
- The Pug has a short glossy coat that sheds. Owners must be prepared to deal with dog hair around the house, although this can be minimized by regular brushing and combing to rid the coat of dead hair.
- Regular grooming, including bathing as needed, is needed to keep the Pug's coat healthy and looking its shiny best.
- Grooming also entails taking care of the eyes, ears, nails, feet and anal glands.

Keeping the Pug Active

Because the Pug is a toy dog, he does not require as much exercise as many other breeds. Nonetheless, some form of regular activity is very important. This is necessary to keep the muscles in good condition as well as to stimulate the brain. A Pug loves to investigate new places and new smells. This keeps his senses alert and probably gives him wonderful things to dream about in those hours of deep doggie sleep.

Many Pugs, when trained, are fairly obedient off lead. However, you

Most Pugs will accept as much exercise as you offer, though not too much.

must always keep foremost in your mind that this is a small breed, so accidents might just happen if larger, heavier dogs are encountered, even more so if your Pug decides to stand his ground against them! Likewise, you don't want to risk your Pug's wandering off to investigate something that catches his fancy, so "on lead only" is a good rule of thumb when out in public.

Life with a Pug is like a day at the beach! This is an easily portable dog that enjoys new experiences with his owners.

A Pug kept as an "only pet" should ideally have at least one short walk each day. If he has other canine company and a large yard in which to exercise, he may be happy enough to go on outings less frequently. The short-faced Pug will not do well with too-strenuous activity. As a sidebar, your Pug should not be left damp following exercise in inclement weather.

If your Pug takes to obedience training, you may like to compete with him. Jumps for small dogs are set up to be proportionate to the dogs' size.

Some Pugs are now used in therapy work, visiting nursing homes and hospitals to meet and share a cuddle with the people there. The breed's convenient size, charming looks and endearing personality make these visits something to which hospital patients and the elderly greatly look forward. It is also not unknown for a Pug to become a "hearing dog." This is a dog that is specially trained to listen for sounds like telephones and doorbells ringing,

Conformation showing is a popular competitive venue for Pugs and their people.

which is of great assistance to an owner with impaired hearing.

In some countries Pugs take part in obedience trials, but it has to be said that the Pug is not a breed that springs immediately to mind when one thinks of agility trials. However, many clubs offer agility trials suited to small breeds, meaning that the obstacles are reduced in size for the smaller dogs. Breeds such as the Pug do not have to compete against larger, quicker ones like the Border Collie.

Even if your Pug does not take part in any organized activities, you can enjoy endless hours of fun together. Keeping your Pug active helps him stay at a healthy weight. When not sleeping or relaxing, he will enjoy games with you and playing with his safe toys. Remember, though, that toys for Pugs should not of the "tugging variety," and all of his toys should be checked regularly to ensure that no loose or small parts could cause accidental harm.

KEEPING THE PUG ACTIVE

Overview

- The short-faced Pug does not need strenuous exercise, but does need activity nonetheless to keep him healthy, in good shape and at a proper weight.
- Daily walks and romps around the yard are good for a Pug. Always keep him on lead or in a secure area when outdoors.
- Look into the activities and events you can do with your Pug, such as pet therapy work, obedience and agility training or maybe dog shows.
- The type of activity that your Pug will enjoy most is anything that the two of you do together.

Your Pug and His Vet

Your Pug is almost certain to cause comment and arouse interest when he visits the vet. Remember, though, that he may be taking a trip there because he is feeling off-color, rather than just for a routine check-up, and may not feel up to extra attention. Your Pug should be either crated or kept on your lap in the waiting room. This will give him reassurance and help to keep him calm. If he is feeling a little under the weather, he will probably not take kindly to larger dogs nosing

Your vet will manage all details of your pup's vaccinations, including which vaccines the pup gets, how frequently he is vaccinated and the booster-shot schedule.

at him on the waiting-room floor.

It is sensible to make early contact with your vet, in part to build up rapport for any subsequent visits. Obviously, if your puppy's course of vaccinations is not yet complete, you will need to take him to the vet in any case, but it is a good idea to take him for a thorough check-up within a day or so of bringing him home.

Regular eye checks are especially important with a breed like the Pug, as the large, round eyes can be vulnerable to problems.

If you do not already have a vet, take recommendations from someone else who owns dogs and whose opinion you trust. Location is also an important factor, for you must be able to get your dog there quickly in an emergency and the vet must be able to respond rapidly when needed. If you live in a rural area, be sure that you choose a vet who has plenty of dealings with small animals. Many have a great deal of experience with farm animals but, sadly, their experience with dogs is limited, something I have learned painfully.

One of the first noticeable signs of a dog's aging is graying around the muzzle. Senior dogs need more frequent visits to the vet for proactive health care.

VACCINATIONS

Routine vaccinations will vary slightly depending upon the area in which you live and the type of vaccine used by your particular vet. Your vet will advise you exactly about timing, when your dog can be exercised in public places after the course of vaccines is complete and when boosters are due. Many vets now send reminder notes for boosters, but you should still make notes on your calendar. If boosters become overdue, it will probably be necessary to start the full vaccination program again. If you are visiting your vet for an initial vaccination program, do not allow your Pug to come into close contact with other dogs in the waiting room, nor indeed on the waiting-room floor!

Some people prefer not to subject their dogs to routine vaccinations, but opt for homeopathic alternatives. This needs to be carried out to the letter, so you must be guided by a vet who also practices homeopathy. Keep in mind that it will probably be difficult to find a boarding kennel that accepts dogs without proof of routine conventional vaccinations. Vaccine protocol varies with many veterinarians, but most recommend a series of three "combination" shots given at three- to four-week intervals. Your puppy should have had his first shot before he left his breeder, and the vet will pick up where the breeder left off.

"Combination" shots vary, and a single injection may contain five, six, seven or even eight vaccines in one shot. Many vets feel the potency in high-combination vaccines can negatively compromise a puppy's immature immune system. They recommend fewer vaccines in one shot or even separating vaccines into individual injections. The wisest and most conservative course is to administer only one shot in a single visit, rather than two or three shots at the same time.

PREVENTATIVE CARE

If your puppy has been bought from a truly dedicated breeder, all necessary care will have been provided for not only the litter but also the dam. She will have had genetic testing, regular health checks and boosters, with a worming routine. These will stand her puppies in good stead and provide them with greater immunity and a healthier start than would otherwise be the case.

CHECK-UPS

When your Pug goes along to the vet for booster vaccinations, your vet will also perform a routine exam and overall check-up. The vet will give your Pug an overall exam, including checking his heart, eyes, ears, teeth and vital signs. If your dog is past middle age, blood tests and other tests may be done, and your veterinarian may suggest more frequent visits.

NEUTERING AND SPAYING

Whether or not you decide to have your dog spayed or

Made in the shade! Owners of short-faced breeds like the Pug have to be extra-cautious about keeping their dogs cool in hot weather.

neutered is a matter of personal choice. In any event, please never allow a vet to spay your bitch until after her first season. Timing "mid-season" will usually be advised.

Should you decide to opt for neutering your male dog or spaying your bitch, you will have to take special care with subsequent weight control. In some cases, an aggressive or over-dominant male can be easier to cope with after neutering, but this is by no means always the case.

Obviously, there are some reasons of ill health that necessitate such operations, particularly pyometra, which will usually require a bitch's ovaries to be removed. In the case of a male with only one or neither testicle descended into the scrotum, your vet may well advise castration to prevent the likelihood of cancer. Discuss all of the pros and cons of the procedure with your vet to help you make the best decision.

YOUR PUG AND HIS VET

Overview

- Choose a vet whom you trust and with whom you feel comfortable; also, the vet should be located nearby in case of emergencies.
- Your vet will manage all aspects of your Pug puppy's vaccination schedule as well as his annual boosters throughout his life.
- Your pup starts out in the best health if bred from healthy parents.
- Your adult Pug will see the vet annually for thorough check-ups, more often as a senior.
- Discuss the pros and cons of neutering/spaying with your breeder and vet to help you make a decision.